PICTURE WINDOW BOOKS
a capstone imprint

Editor: Julie Gassman
Designer: Ashlee Suker
Art Director: Nathan Gassman
Production Specialist: Laura Manthe
The illustrations in this book were created with watercolor.

Picture Window Books
1710 Roe Crest Drive
North Mankato, MN 56003
www.capstonepub.com

Library of Congress Cataloging-in-Publication Data
Manushkin, Fran.
  What happens next, Katie?: writing a narrative with Katie Woo / by
Fran Manushkin; illustrated by Tammie Lyon.
       p. cm. — (Katie Woo, star writer)
  Includes sidebars about writing a story and the differences between
fiction and nonfiction.
  Summary: When Katie and her family go on a trip, she decides to write
a story for her friends to show how much she misses them.
ISBN 978-1-4048-8129-7 (library binding)
ISBN 978-1-4795-1924-8 (paperback)
ISBN 978-1-4795-1890-6 (eBook PDF)
1. Woo, Katie (Fictitious character)—Juvenile fiction. 2. Chinese
Americans—Juvenile fiction. 3. Fiction—Authorship—Juvenile fiction. 4.
Creative writing—Juvenile fiction. 5. Friendship—Juvenile fiction.
[1. Chinese Americans—Fiction. 2. Fiction—Authorship—Fiction. 3.
Creative writing—Fiction. 4. Friendship—Fiction.] I. Lyon, Tammie, ill.
II. Title.

PZ7.M3195Whe 2013
813.54—dc23   2013004210

Katie Woo

star writer

What Happens Next, Katie?

Writing a Narrative with Katie Woo

by Fran Manushkin

illustrated by Tammie Lyon

Katie was going on a trip.

"I'll miss you," said JoJo.

"Me too!" said Pedro.

"I wish you were coming with me,"

sighed Katie.

"I have an idea," said JoJo. "Why don't you write a story about your trip? When we read it, we can feel like we took the trip too."

"That's a great idea," agreed Pedro. "Katie's stories are fun!"

Katie's Star Tip

Another word for story is *narrative*. When you write a narrative, you are telling a story. I love telling friends about exciting or surprising things that happen. I like making people laugh, so my stories are funny. If you write a story down, it can last forever!

"Remember your story about

Halloween?" said JoJo. "You thought

you saw a ghost!"

"Scary stories are fun," said Pedro.

Katie's dad called, "Hurry, Katie!
It's time to pack for our trip."

"Okay," said Katie. "I hope I don't
forget anything."

"Don't forget to write your story,"
said JoJo.

"I won't!" Katie promised.

Katie packed her suitcase and took some money out of her piggybank.

"I may need it," she said. "You never know."

Then it was time to go.

"Good-bye, house!" Katie shouted.

"See you next week."

"I love trips!" said Katie. "You never know what is going to happen. I hope it is something exciting!"

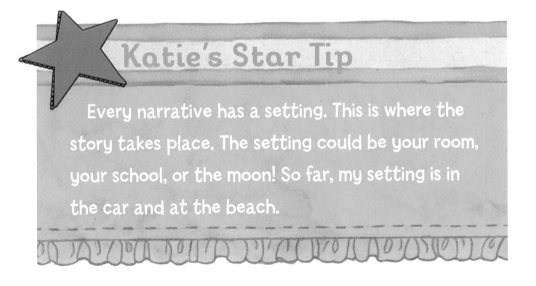

Katie's Star Tip

Every narrative has a setting. This is where the story takes place. The setting could be your room, your school, or the moon! So far, my setting is in the car and at the beach.

"I can't wait to see the beach," said Katie's dad. "I love to smell the salty air."

"I like writing words in the shiny sand," said Katie. "And watching the waves erase them."

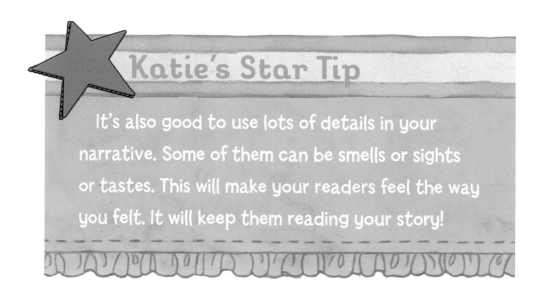

Katie's Star Tip

It's also good to use lots of details in your narrative. Some of them can be smells or sights or tastes. This will make your readers feel the way you felt. It will keep them reading your story!

"Our beach is on an island,"
explained Katie's dad. "We must take
a boat there."

"Uh-oh!" moaned Katie's mom.
"We've missed the boat! We'll have to
wait for the next one."

"My story will be exciting!" said
Katie. "So far we have a missing boat.
I wonder what will
happen next?"

"It's starting to rain!" said Katie's mom.

It rained and rained!

"Rain is good for the trees and the flowers," said Katie's mom.

"But not for the beach," sighed Katie. "Maybe my story will be a sad one."

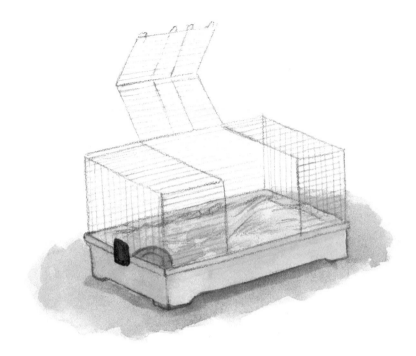

"Some stories are sad," said Katie's

dad. "I remember the one you wrote

about your guinea pig. It started out

sad when Binky got lost."

"That's right," agreed Katie. "But then I found Binky, and my story had a happy ending."

Katie's Star Tip

Every narrative has a mood. The mood is how a story makes your readers feel. Losing a pet makes for a sad mood. Finding him again makes things happy!

"I remember another happy story," said Katie's mom. "It was the one you wrote about the Fourth of July."

"That was a fun story," said Katie. "Fireworks make a story sparkle!"

Finally it stopped
raining, and the sun
came out. The boat
came too. "Beach, here
we come!" sang Katie. "Now
we'll have fun!"

"Oh, no!" said Katie's dad. "I forgot my wallet. We don't have any money!"

"Don't worry!" said Katie's mom. "I have some."

"Me too!" said Katie. "I took money out of my piggy bank. We'll have plenty of money for ice cream."

Katie went swimming in
the cool, salty sea and
waved at the noisy

seagulls. She made a

fancy sand castle too.

But she missed her friends. "I wish

Pedro and JoJo were here,"

she sighed.

"It's getting very hot," said
Katie's mom.

"I know how to feel cooler," said
Katie. "I won't write a story about
the beach. I'll write a make-believe
story about a cold, icy place."

Katie's Star Tip

There are two kinds of narratives: If I write a
true story about what happens on my trip, it's
called nonfiction. But since I've decided to write
a make-believe story, that is called fiction. Both
kinds of stories are fun to write and read!

"I'll put Pedro and JoJo in my story," Katie decided. "Then I won't miss them so much."

Katie's Star Tip

Pedro and JoJo are going to be characters in my narrative. The characters can be people, animals, or creatures, like monsters! The main character is the most important character in the story because he or she talks and does the most. I think I will be the main character in my story.

Katie told her mom and dad, "In my story, Pedro and JoJo and I will dig a big hole."

"Really?" said her dad. "What happens next?"

Katie smiled. "We will stand upside down on the other side of the world! I've always wanted to do that."

"What happens next?" asked
Katie's mom.

"A big blizzard, that's what!"
said Katie. "Our noses
will turn pink and icicles
will grow on them!"

"Brr!" said Katie's dad.
"Then what happens?"

"I don't know," said Katie. "I'm
still thinking."

Katie grabbed her notebook and pencil. "I know!" she decided. "I'll add wild animals! They are always fun in a story."

Katie had a great time making up adventures. Here is her story:

JoJo and Pedro and I dug a hole
to the other side of the world.
"Wow!" I said, shivering. "It's cold
and snowy here!"

Suddenly, Pedro yelled, "Watch out!
Here comes a polar bear."

"Oh, no!" I cried. "He wants to eat
us up!"

"No way!" yelled JoJo. "I see a whale.
Maybe he can help!"

Katie's Star Tip

My teacher, Miss Winkle, says that we should use temporal words in our narratives. These are words that tell us about time. I used the temporal words *suddenly*, *then*, and *while* in my story.

"Oh, Mr. Whale," I shouted, "we don't want to be the bear's supper. Can we jump onto your big, shiny back?"

"Sure!" the whale spouted. "Hop on! I was so lonely, and now I have three new friends."

Then the whale sang a happy song while he floated us home. And the best part was nobody ate us up!

Katie's Star Tip

Sometimes the characters in the story can help tell it. When a character talks, that is called dialogue. In my story, Pedro, JoJo, the whale, and I all talk. Don't forget to use quotation marks around the words your characters say. Then your readers will know one of the characters is talking.

When Katie got home, she read her story. "That was cool," said Pedro. "In every way."

"For sure," agreed JoJo. "I'm glad you didn't forget about us."

"No way!" said Katie. "Now let's go skating. One, two, three—go!"

Off they raced, all afternoon! But that is another story.

Write Your Own Narrative!

Writing naratives is so much fun! You can write about nonfiction things that really happened, or you can write a fictional story and make everything up! Here are some ideas to get you started:

- ❀ Write about your last birthday celebration. Include lots of details about the party.

- ❀ Imagine you got lost at the mall. What happens to you? Write a story about it.

- ❀ Write about a time that you tried something new. How did you feel?

- ❀ Pretend you are an animal, and write a story about what your days are like.

- ❀ Think about a day when something really important happened to you, like you got a pet or you moved. Write about it.

- ❀ Write a story about a trip to Mars.

Glossary

character—a person, animal, or creature in a narrative

detail—one of many facts about a certain thing

dialogue—words spoken between two or more characters; in writing, dialogue is set off with quotation marks

fiction—something that is made up or untrue

main character—the most important character in a narrative; main characters speak and act more than other characters

mood—the way that you are feeling

narrative—a story that is told or written

nonfiction—something that is true

setting—the time and place of a narrative

temporal word—a word that tells about time or when things happen

Read More

Fandel, Jennifer. *You Can Write Awesome Stories.* You Can Write. North Mankato, Minn.: Capstone Press, 2012.

Minden, Cecilia and Kate Roth. *How to Write about Your Adventure.* Language Arts Explorer Junior. Ann Arbor, Mich.: Cherry Lake Pub., 2012.

Stone, Janet. *How to Tell a Legend.* Text Styles. New York: Crabtree Pub. Co., 2012.

On the Internet

✿ Learn more about Katie and her friends.

✿ Find a Katie Woo color sheet, scrapbook, and stationery.

✿ Discover more Katie Woo books.

All at ... www.capstonekids.com

Still Want More?
Find cool websites related to this book at *www.facthound.com.*

Just type in this code: **9781404881297** and you're ready to go!

About the Author

Fran Manushkin is the author of many popular picture books, including *Baby, Come Out!*; *Latkes and Applesauce: A Hanukkah Story*; *The Tushy Book*; *The Belly Book*; and *Big Girl Panties*. There is a real Katie Woo—she's Fran's great-niece—but she never gets in half the trouble of the Katie Woo in the books. Fran writes on her beloved Mac computer in New York City, without the help of her two naughty cats, Chaim and Goldy.

About the Illustrator

Tammie Lyon began her love for drawing at a young age while sitting at the kitchen table with her dad. She continued her love of art and eventually attended the Columbus College of Art and Design, where she earned a bachelor's degree in fine art. Today she lives with her husband, Lee, in Cincinnati, Ohio. Her dogs, Gus and Dudley, keep her company as she works in her studio.

Look for all the books in the series: